DESIGN YOUR FUTURE

CAREERS

TO HELP OTHERS

Shantel Gobin

Rourke

T0008867

Before Reading: *Building Background Knowledge and Vocabulary*

Building background knowledge can help children process new information and build upon what they already know. Before reading a book, it is important to tap into what children already know about the topic. This will help them develop their vocabulary and increase their reading comprehension.

Questions and Activities to Build Background Knowledge:

1. Look at the front cover of the book and read the title. What do you think this book will be about?
2. What do you already know about this topic?
3. Take a book walk and skim the pages. Look at the table of contents, photographs, captions, and bold words. Did these text features give you any information or predictions about what you will read in this book?

Vocabulary: *Vocabulary Is Key to Reading Comprehension*

Use the following directions to prompt a conversation about each word.

- Read the vocabulary words.
- What comes to mind when you see each word?
- What do you think each word means?

Vocabulary Words:

- certification
- consular
- embassies
- licensing
- practicum
- rehabilitation

During Reading: *Reading for Meaning and Understanding*

To achieve deep comprehension of a book, children are encouraged to use close reading strategies. During reading, it is important to have children stop and make connections. These connections result in deeper analysis and understanding of a book.

Close Reading a Text

During reading, have children stop and talk about the following:

- Any confusing parts
- Any unknown words
- Text to text, text to self, text to world connections
- The main idea in each chapter or heading

Encourage children to use context clues to determine the meaning of any unknown words. These strategies will help children learn to analyze the text more thoroughly as they read.

When you are finished reading this book, turn to the next-to-last page for **After-Reading Questions** and an **Activity**.

TABLE OF CONTENTS

Your interests can start you on the path to a job you'll love. Do you like to lend a helping hand? Are you a people person? A career helping others may be just right! Let's explore different career paths that all lead to a life of making a difference.

Keep an eye out for these icons to learn more about how to achieve your goals:

 Minimum education/training required

 Average time commitment (beyond a high school diploma or GED)

 Ways to boost your qualifications

DENTAL HYGIENIST

Tooth be told, everyone wants a set of pearly white teeth. Dental hygienists help people do just that! Cleaning teeth is only part of the job. Looking for signs of health issues in the mouth is another way they help patients. Dental hygienists also teach patients how to take care of their own teeth to prevent problems. Most work in a dentist's office. But there are some unique options, such as working in a mobile dental clinic or correctional facility.

Associate's degree
Pass a **licensing** exam

2–3 years

Bachelor's degree in dental hygiene

licensing (LYE-suhns-ing): authorizing someone to do something, such as practice medicine

CERTIFIED NURSING ASSISTANT

If you are interested in nursing but not sure if college is for you, becoming a certified nursing assistant may be the perfect fit! Nursing assistants help nurses take care of patients' daily needs. This can mean obtaining vital signs, changing linens, or bathing patients. These professionals can work in places such as hospitals or **rehabilitation** centers. Since they play a major role in aiding patients who can no longer take care of their own needs, many certified nursing assistants work in nursing homes and adult care centers.

Certification program

4–8 weeks

Associate's degree in nursing

certification (sur-tuh-fuh-KAY-shuhn): the process of earning an official document that states that special qualifications within a field have been met

rehabilitation (ree-uh-bil-uh-TAY-shuhn): the restoration of someone, especially by therapeutic means, to an improved condition

OCCUPATIONAL THERAPIST

Occupational therapists help people of all ages use their own skills to get things done in their everyday lives. They work with individuals who have a disability, illness, or injury. Their job varies depending on who they are helping. An occupational therapist may help a child with fine-motor problems learn how to hold a pair of scissors. They can help someone recovering from an accident learn how to feed themselves all over again. If someone needs a walking aid to get around, an occupational therapist could teach them how to use a walker safely.

Master's degree

6 years

Supervised fieldwork
Pass a licensing exam

Occupational therapists can work anywhere people need them. They can go to clients in places such as hospitals, rehabilitation centers, and nursing homes. Some can even work in schools or right in people's homes! They can also have clients come to them in places such as clinics and private offices.

Hacks & Hints

If you know occupational therapy is what you want to do, look for a college that offers a fast-track program. Often called 4+1, 4+2, or accelerated programs, they allow you to complete the educational requirements faster by combining the bachelor's and master's degree into one program. Instead of 6 or more years, you could be finished in as soon as 4.5!

TEACHER OF ENGLISH AS A FOREIGN LANGUAGE

This is not your average teaching job. Teachers of English as a foreign language travel around the world helping non-English speakers learn English. While most of them relocate to work in the countries where their students are, some teach online. As you might guess, many of these professionals work in schools teaching grades K–12. But they can also work for charity organizations such as the Peace Corps, as tutors in private homes, or for universities.

Certification program in teaching English as a foreign language
Bachelor's degree (required in most countries)

4 years

Practicum hours
Bachelor's degree in education

practicum (PRAK-ti-kum):
a course a student takes
that involves applying the
lessons learned within the
course to the real world
under trained supervision

FLIGHT ATTENDANT

"Ladies and gentlemen, please fasten your seatbelts." Flight attendants help people stay safe and comfortable while traveling on a plane. Some of their most important tasks are inspecting safety equipment and showing passengers what to do in case of an emergency. They also make sure people follow the rules during the flight. Flight attendants take care of passengers' basic needs as well by providing food and drinks.

GED or high school diploma

Certification program

At least 20/40 vision (with or without contacts or glasses)

3–6 weeks

Associate's or bachelor's degree

Foreign language skills

CONSULAR OFFICER

A **consular** officer works for the United States (US) government in **embassies** all around the world. Their job is to help US citizens handle problems while in another country. This can be as simple as replacing a lost passport or as complicated as helping someone get out of jail. They also help with important documents, such as adoption papers and visas.

VISA APPLICATION

consular (KAHN-suh-ler): relating to someone who has been officially appointed by a government to live in a foreign country and represent the home country

embassies (EM-buh-seez): official places in a foreign country where an ambassador works

U.S. Embassy London

- GED or high school diploma

- No set time

- Advanced degrees (bachelor's or master's)
  Foreign language skills

Consular officers can be put in high stress situations. If a country becomes too dangerous for American citizens and their allies, it is the job of the consular officer to evacuate them. Problem-solving skills and the ability to stay calm under pressure are great attributes for this position.

Hacks & Hints

While there are no secondary education requirements to be a consular officer, it might be worth your while to get a degree. Pay is based on experience and degree level, so if you hold an advanced degree, you immediately have a leg up.

EVENT PLANNER

Can you say, "Best party ever"? Event planners help people organize important events. From birthday parties to weddings to business meetings, if it's an event that can be planned, an event planner can plan it! Their job will vary depending on the client. It can include arranging the location, food, cost, and transportation. When the day comes, event planners are in charge of making sure everything goes off without a hitch.

 GED or high school diploma

No set time

Work for an event planner
Bachelor's degree

FUNERAL DIRECTOR

Help is needed from beginning to end. Funeral directors help families put loved ones to rest by planning and managing the details of a funeral. This can include scheduling services, arranging transportation, and handling the body of the deceased. Funeral directors can provide extra support by filing death certificates and other paperwork, as well as directing families to counseling services.

Requirements vary by state
Associate's degree
Pass a licensing exam

2 years

Apprenticeship

PERSONAL TRAINER

Personal trainers help people of all ages get and stay in good physical shape. First, they create a unique plan for each client to reach their fitness goals. Then, they help them get there! Demonstrating and monitoring exercises is a must in this job. Educating clients on the purpose of each exercise and motivating them to complete the routine are also important duties. Some personal trainers also help clients with nutrition plans.

GED or high school diploma

No set time

Certification in personal training

Commonly, personal trainers work in gyms, fitness clubs, or people's homes. Many also train in outdoor spaces, like parks or fields. Some are hired by companies to work with their employees in an office space. Those with more training or education may get positions working with sports teams.

MEMORY GAME

Look at the pictures. What do you remember reading on the page where each image appeared?

INDEX

AFTER—READING QUESTIONS

1. Which career path can lead you to having your hands in someone's mouth?
2. Who helps people after a loved one has died?
3. Who would you call to throw the best party ever?
4. What does an occupational therapist do?
5. What career requires good vision?

ACTIVITY

Imagine you are going to interview one of the professionals you just learned about. Write a list of questions you would like to ask them about their job. Do some research and see if you can find the answers to your questions!

ABOUT THE AUTHOR

Shantel Gobin loves helping people grow and achieve their goals. She enjoys writing to inspire new ways of thinking. It is her goal to create a generation of lifelong learners. She lives in Brooklyn, New York, where she works as a school psychologist and author.

© 2023 Rourke Educational Media

All rights reserved. No part of this book may be reproduced or utilized in any form or by any means, electronic or mechanical including photocopying, recording, or by any information storage and retrieval system without permission in writing from the publisher.

www.rourkebooks.com

PHOTO CREDITS: cover, title page: ©RaiDztor/ Shutterstock.com, ©marekuliasz/ Shutterstock.com, ©Tomislav Pinter/ Shutterstock.com, ©aldomurillo/ Getty Images, ©supersizer/ Getty Images, ©FangXiaNuo/ Getty Images; title page, pages 4-6, 10-13, 15-17, 19-22, 26-30: ©Flas100/ Shutterstock.com; TOC, pages 4-32: ©RaiDztor/ Shutterstock.com; TOC, pages 4, 6, 14, 30-32: ©My Life Graphic/ Shutterstock.com; pages 8-9, 14-15, 18-19: ©marekuliasz/ Shutterstock.com; pages 4, 6, 8, 10, 14, 16, 19, 22, 24, 26: ©13ree.design/ Shutterstock.com; pages 7, 17: ©Netalieh/ Getty Images; pages 9, 21 ,23: ©belterz/ Getty Images; pages 4, 6-12, 14, 16, 17, 19, 22, 24, 26: ©MichaelJayBerlin/ Shutterstock.com; pages 7, 23: ©Realstockvector/ Shutterstock.com; pages 4-5: ©FatCamera/ Getty Images; pages 6-7: ©gpointstudio/ Shutterstock.com; page 7: ©michaeljung/ Shutterstock.com; page 8: ©onair/ Shutterstock.com; pages 8-9: ©entreguin/ Shutterstock.com; page 9: ©PeopleImages/ Getty Images; page 11: ©aldomurillo/ Getty Images, ©damircudic/ Getty Images; page 12: ©sturti/ Getty Images; page 13: ©Mario Arango/ Getty Images; pages 14-15, 30: ©CHINE NOUVELLE/SIPA/Newscom; page 15: ©Prostock-studio/ Shutterstock.com; pages 16-17: ©Hispanolistic/ Getty Images; pages 15, 30: ©Svitlana Hulko/ Getty Images; pages 18-19: ©Willy Barton/ Shutterstock.com; pages 18-19, 30: ©Motortion/ Getty Images; pages 20-21: ©Mass Communication Specialist 1st Class Nathan Carpenter; page 21: ©POOL/REUTERS/Newscom; page 23: ©LumiNola/ Getty Images; pages 22-23, 30: ©svetikd/ Getty Images; pages 24-25, 30: ©Nikola Stojadinovic/ Getty Images; pages 27, 30: ©SDI Productions/ Getty Images; page 28: ©bbernard/ Shutterstock.com; pages 28-29: ©nattrass/ Getty Images; page 29: ©DisobeyArt/ Shutterstock.com

Edited by: Hailey Scragg
Cover and interior design by: Alison Tracey

Library of Congress PCN Data

Careers to Help Others / Shantel Gobin
(Design Your Future)
ISBN 978-1-73165-284-3 (hard cover)
ISBN 978-1-73165-254-6 (soft cover)
ISBN 978-1-73165-314-7 (e-book)
ISBN 978-1-73165-344-4 (e-pub)
Library of Congress Control Number: 2021952198

Rourke Educational Media
Printed in the United States of America
01-2412211937